ZOMBIE WASPS

Written by Mike Gould

Contents

Collins

It's a jungle out there

MONSTER SPIDER...CRAWLING TERROR 100 FEET HIGH!

RESEARCHERS SEEKING CLUE!

CAN ANYTHING ESCAPE IT?

TARANTULA!

STARRING JOHN AGAR · MARA CORDAY · LEO G. CARROLL

There are lots of films about creepy-crawlies, some of them scarier than others! But there are bugs everywhere, including in your garden. Have you spotted any?

2

"Bug" is a common word for "insect".

All insects have a three-part body:

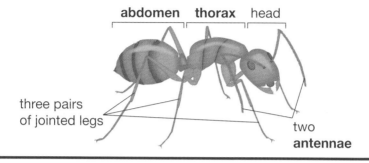

abdomen   thorax   head

three pairs
of jointed legs

two
antennae

The scare scale

Some people are more scared of bugs than others.

Where are *you* on the scare scale?

terrified

very scared

quite scared

don't like them

OK

not scared at all!

3

Scary stingers

Bees, ants and wasps are all insects that sting.

Asian giant hornets

Asian giant hornets have
a stinger that's six millimetres long –
about the length of an ant.
That might not sound like much,
but their sting can be deadly.
In Japan, these bugs kill more people than all other
creatures put together, including wild bears!

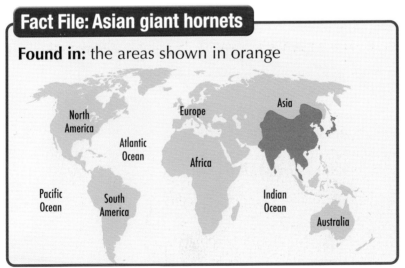

Fact File: Asian giant hornets

Found in: the areas shown in orange

North America
Europe
Asia
Atlantic Ocean
Africa
Pacific Ocean
South America
Indian Ocean
Australia

Zombie wasps

You might have heard of the fictional creatures called zombies – dead things that are brought back to life. But did you know that there are zombie wasps?

A female wasp injects its egg into the body of another insect, such as a ladybird.

The **larva** hatches from the egg and eats the ladybird's insides. Then the larva emerges through the ladybird's abdomen.

The wasp stings the ladybird with **venom** to stun it. The ladybird twitches like a zombie, but can't move itself.

5

Tarantula hawk wasps

Tarantula hawk wasps eat
tarantula spiders.

A hawk wasp will grab one of the spider's legs with its jaws.
When the spider tries to fight back, the wasp stings it
until it stops moving. Then the wasp drags the spider off
to its nest and lays an egg on it. The egg turns into larva,
which feed on the spider.

The Schmidt sting pain index

Scientist Justin Schmidt created a scale from one to four to measure how bad stings are. He let lots of different bugs sting or bite him to decide where each bug was on the scale!

Sweat bees have one of the least painful stings, rated at 1.0 on the scale. Justin said it "feels as if a tiny spark has **singed** a single hair on your arm."

Justin put honey bees at 2.0, with their sting feeling like a match burning your skin.

Tarantula hawk wasps are at the top of the scale, at 4.0. Justin Schmidt described their sting as "blinding, fierce, shockingly electric".

Giant bugs

Most people think bugs are small, but some of them are huge.

Hercules moths

Hercules moths have a wingspan of around 27 centimetres – about the length of a piece of A4 paper.

The moths get their name from Hercules, a character from Roman legend.

He was very big and strong, just like Hercules moths.

Titan longhorn beetles

Titan longhorns have the longest bodies of all beetles.
They can measure nearly 17 centimetres including their
jaws and horns – that's about
the length of a pencil.

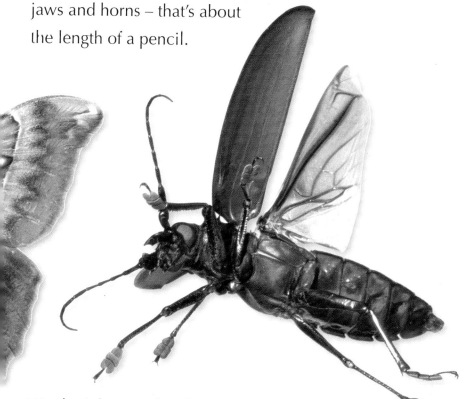

We don't know a lot about these bugs, but
it's believed that adult males don't eat. Instead, they
survive on the food they ate when they were **larvae**.

Titan longhorn beetles hiss when they're scared and their
jaws are strong enough to snap a pencil in half.

Giant centipedes

Giant centipedes are the world's biggest centipedes. They can grow up to 30 centimetres – around the size of a recorder.

Giant centipedes can kill **prey** that's 15 times their size, thanks to the nasty venom in their claws.

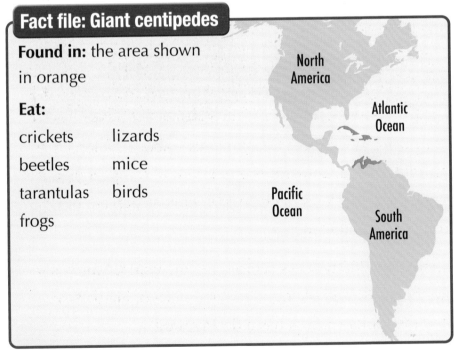

Fact file: Giant centipedes

Found in: the area shown in orange

Eat:

crickets	lizards
beetles	mice
tarantulas	birds
frogs	

North America

Atlantic Ocean

Pacific Ocean

South America

Emperor scorpions

Emperor scorpions are the world's biggest scorpions. They are found in West Africa, and live in burrows with up to 20 others!

a mother carrying her young on her back

They can grow up to 23 centimetres – about the length of an adult's hand. Emperor scorpions don't sting much, but use their giant claws to crush their prey, which are mostly beetles and millipedes.

There are 1700 types of scorpion in the world. Watch out for the death **stalker**, found in the deserts of North Africa and the Middle East. It has a deadly sting!

Armies, swarms and fighters

One nasty bug can be a problem – but sometimes they come in armies of thousands!

Ants

Ants work, live and fight together.

In an ant **colony** you will find:

- the queen – her job is to lay eggs
- male ants – they don't do much except mate and die
- worker ants – they are female and protect the queen, find food and fight off enemy ants from other colonies.

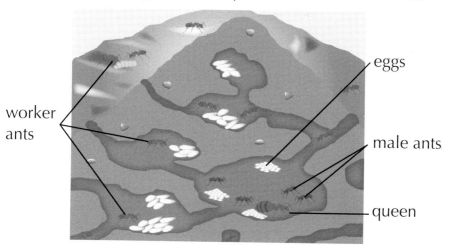

worker ants

eggs

male ants

queen

Did you know?

- Some of the worker ants are soldier ants, which have bigger heads and huge **mandibles** to fight and kill.

- Some soldier ants' heads are the same shape as the hole leading to their nest. This means they can use their heads to block the hole and stop enemies getting in.

- A few types of ants steal eggs from other colonies, then make the ants that hatch from the eggs work for them!

Warlike termites

Warlike termites look similar to ants, but they have very different nests. They create big mounds of earth with a tunnel running up through the centre.

Several million termites live in each mound. They are all children of a king and queen who live inside.

The queen lays about 30,000 eggs a day. That's around ten million each year!

The termites live for about one year, apart from the king and queen, who can live for over 20 years. That's a lot of eggs!

a queen termite filled with eggs

Bullet ants

Bullet ants are some of the world's largest ants and are found in Central and South America.

They are real fighters – if you're stung by a bullet ant, it feels as if you've been shot. Justin Schmidt rated bullet ants 4.0 on his sting pain index (see page 7).

Did you know?

Bullet ants are sometimes called "24 hour ants" because it can take 24 hours for the pain of their sting to wear off.

Killer bees

Killer bees were created in an experiment in Brazil. The plan was to mate European honey bees with African bees to create super bees that would make more honey. However, some of the African bees escaped and mated with local bees instead. This created killer bees, which attack people in huge swarms.

When one of these bees stings you, it lets out a special banana-like smell. This tells other bees to attack and hundreds can sting you at once. These killer bees have spread from Brazil to the USA and have killed over 1000 people so far.

Did you know?
People still use killer bees to produce honey!

17

Hidden horrors

Some insects can be hard to spot. They use their colour or shape to blend in with the background.

We call this camouflage – like the clothes that nature photographers or soldiers often wear.

photographer wearing camouflage to get close to an animal

Insects camouflage themselves to hide from their enemies or to sneak up on their prey.

Can you see the insect in each of these pictures?

Giant Asian mantises

Giant Asian mantises are the same colour as the leaves around them, so they're very hard to spot!

You wouldn't want to be a nearby mouse, tree frog or lizard – these mantises eat them all.

The females eat their male partners, too! They often attack, kill and eat males just after they've mated.

Fact file: Giant Asian mantises

Found in: the area shown in orange

Body size: females up to nine centimetres, males up to eight centimetres

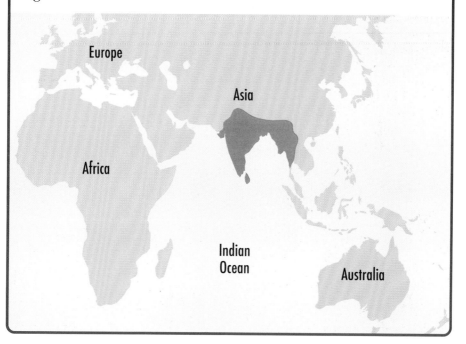

Europe

Asia

Africa

Indian
Ocean

Australia

Did you know?

Giant Asian mantises have large eyes and can turn their heads 180 degrees – a half circle. This means they can look right behind them. While they do this, the rest of their body stays still!

Wang Lang and the mantis

It is said that **kung-fu** expert Wang Lang learnt some of his best moves from a mantis.

One day, Wang saw a mantis fighting a bigger insect in the woods near his temple.

The mantis won by using its arms to "climb" its opponent.

Wang took the mantis back to the temple and spoke to it. "Maybe you can teach me something," he said.

someone practising a mantis move

Wang used a piece of straw to prod the mantis and watched how the mantis responded.

Wang developed new kung-fu moves based on what the mantis did.

Later, Wang's master returned to the temple, and Wang won against him for the first time.

Together they developed a new form of kung-fu. They called it "Mantis Boxing".

Brown recluse spiders

If you are someone who likes to keep out of people's way, you might be called a recluse.

That is how brown recluse spiders got their name – because they like to keep hidden.

It's a good job that brown recluse spiders keep to themselves, because their bite can kill.

These spiders like anywhere dry and warm, such as sheds, garages and cardboard boxes. However, they have also been found in gloves, shoes and even piles of clothes!

Fact file: Brown recluse spiders

Found in: the area shown in orange

Also called: fiddleback spiders, violin spiders, brown fiddlers

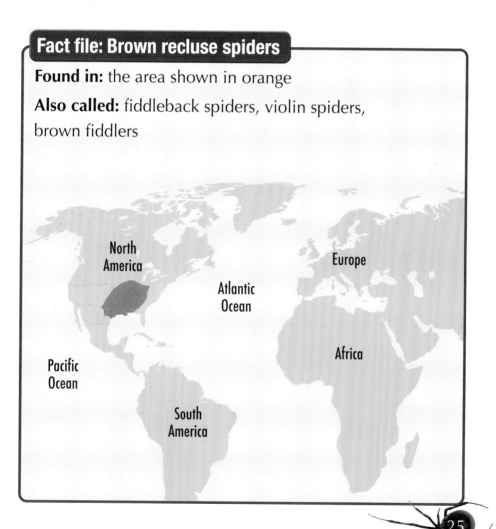

North America

Europe

Atlantic Ocean

Pacific Ocean

Africa

South America

Your worst bug

This book has shown you lots of beastly insects:

- big ones, like giant centipedes

- tiny terrors, like bullet ants

- and monsters, like tarantula hawk wasps.

What do you think makes some bugs really scary? Is it …

- how strong their venom is

- how big they are

- or how clever they are?

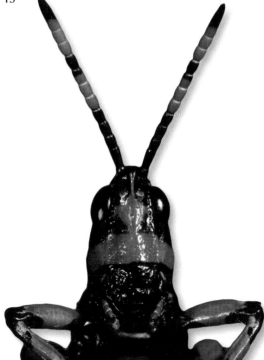

What do you think are the scariest insects?

Perhaps they aren't in this book. Perhaps they haven't even been found yet.

Maybe you can find one yourself! Go out into your garden or into a nearby field or wood. Lift up a branch, or look under some leaves or plants. Will you uncover a monster bug?

Glossary

abdomen the rear part of an insect's body

antennae a pair of long, thin body parts found on the heads of some insects and other animals, used for hearing, smelling and feeling

colony a group of the same type of animals or insects that live together

kung-fu a form of self-defence that comes from China, which uses your hands and feet

larva an insect after it hatches from an egg and before it becomes an adult (plural larvae)

mandibles the jaws of an insect

prey an insect or animal that's hunted for food

singed burnt something a little

stalker someone or something that follows another in a threatening way

thorax the middle part of an insect's body, which holds together the head, legs and wings

venom poison produced by insects, snakes and other animals, put into their prey by biting or stinging

Index

29

Creepy-crawlies big and small

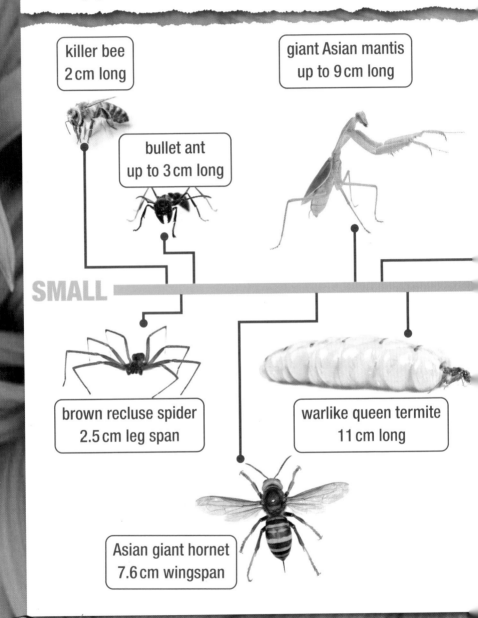

killer bee
2 cm long

giant Asian mantis
up to 9 cm long

bullet ant
up to 3 cm long

SMALL

brown recluse spider
2.5 cm leg span

warlike queen termite
11 cm long

Asian giant hornet
7.6 cm wingspan

tarantula hawk wasp
10 cm wingspan

emperor scorpion
up to 23 cm long

Hercules moth
27 cm wingspan

BIG

giant centipede
30 cm long

titan longhorn beetle
17 cm long

Ideas for reading

Written by Gill Matthews
Primary Literacy Consultant

Reading objectives:
- identify how language, structure and presentation contribute to meaning
- retrieve and record information from non-fiction
- participate in discussion about books, taking turns and listening to what others say

Spoken language objectives:
- articulate and justify answers, arguments and opinions
- use spoken language to develop understanding through speculating, hypothesising, imagining and exploring ideas
- participate in discussion, presentations, performances, role play, improvisations and debates

Curriculum links: Science – Animals, including humans

Interest words: giant, tiny, small, huge, big

Resources: interest words written on individual cards

Build a context for reading
- Show children the front cover of the book. Explore their understanding of the title and discuss what they think a zombie wasp might be like.
- Read the back-cover blurb and ask children what kind of book they think this is.
- Discuss the different features that information books have, for example, contents list, glossary, photographs.
- Ask children to think about the different ways information can be presented in information books, then write them up as a list.

Understand and apply reading strategies
- Ask children to find the contents page, then discuss how it is organised. Then, ask them to find the glossary and index and look at how they are organised.